¡Felices fiestas! / Happy Holidays!

¡FELIZ CUATRO DE JULIO!/ HAPPY FOURTH OF JULY!

By Alex Appleby

Traducción al español: Christina Green

Gareth Stevens Publishing

Contenido

Contents

¡El cuatro de julio celebramos una gran fiesta!

The Fourth of July is a great holiday!

Se celebra en el verano.

It happens
in the summer.

¡Es el cumpleaños
de Estados Unidos!

It is America's birthday!

Las personas hacen grandes fiestas.

People like to have big parties.

Se hacen buenas
comidas al aire libre.

They cook
good food outside.

Please visit our website, www.garethstevens.com. For a free color catalog of all our high-quality books, call toll free 1-800-542-2595 or fax 1-877-542-2596.

Library of Congress Cataloging-in-Publication Data

Appleby, Alex.
Happy Fourth of July! = ¡Feliz Cuatro de Julio! / by Alex Appleby.
p. cm. — (Happy holidays! = ¡Felices fiestas!)
Parallel title: ¡Felices fiestas!
In English and Spanish.
Includes index.
ISBN 978-1-4339-9962-8 (library binding)
1. Fourth of July — Juvenile literature. 2. Fourth of July celebrations — Juvenile literature. I. Appleby, Alex. II. Title.
E286.A66 2014
394.263—d23

First Edition

Published in 2014 by
Gareth Stevens Publishing
111 East 14th Street, Suite 349
New York, NY 10003

Editor: Ryan Nagelhout
Designer: Sarah Liddell
Spanish Translation: Christina Green

Photo credits: Cover, p. 1 (fireworks) Deymos/Shutterstock.com; cover, p. 1 (flag) cdrin/Shutterstock.com; p. 5 Blend Images/Ariel Skelley/the Agency Collection/Getty Images; p. 7 Ariel Skelley/Blend Images/Getty Images; p. 9 Jamie Grill/The Image Bank/Getty Images; p. 11 Hero Images/the Agency Collection/Getty Images; pp. 13, 17 Bochkarev Photography/Shutterstock.com; pp. 15, 24 (grill) Hurst Photo/Shutterstock.com; p. 19 iStock/Thinkstock.com; pp. 21, 24 (fireworks) redswept/Shutterstock.com; p. 23 elen_studio/Shutterstock.com.

Printed in the United States of America

CPSIA compliance information: Batch #CW14GS: For further information contact Gareth Stevens, New York, New York at 1-800-542-2595.

Muchos usan
una parrilla.

Many use a grill.

¡Las personas cocinan perritos calientes!

People make hot dogs!

También les gusta jugar.
Muchos juegan
al béisbol.

They like to play games.
Many people play
baseball.

A las personas les gusta
ver fuegos artificiales.

People like
to set off fireworks.

Son de colores brillantes.

They come in many bright colors.

Palabras que debes saber/ Words to Know

(los) fuegos artificiales/ fireworks

(la) parrilla/ grill

Índice/Index